TABLE OF CONTENTS

Chapter 1

A MYSTERIOUS World

Science as we know it did not exist in the 1600s. There were no labs with computers and high-powered equipment. Schools and colleges did not offer science classes. Imagine how different life was back then. Without science, there were no modern conveniences, no pre-packaged foods, and no life-saving medications.

Many colonists died from illnesses that are curable today.

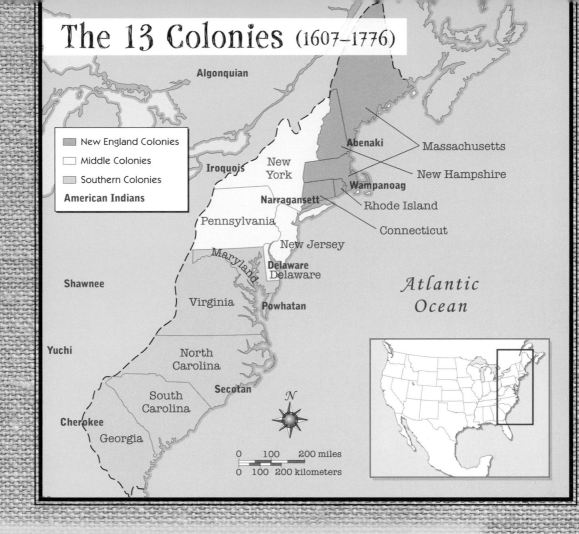

The 13 Colonies (1607–1776)

Algonquian

New England Colonies
Middle Colonies
Southern Colonies
American Indians

Iroquois

New York

Narragansett

Pennsylvania

Maryland

Delaware
Delaware

Shawnee

Virginia

Powhatan

Yuchi

North Carolina

Secotan

South Carolina

Cherokee

Georgia

Abenaki — Massachusetts

— New Hampshire

Wampanoag

— Rhode Island

— Connecticut

New Jersey

Atlantic Ocean

N

0   100   200 miles
0   100 200 kilometers

Of course, people had questions about the world around them. But in the 1600s, there were few scientific answers. Even the most skilled doctors did not know that germs made people sick. They'd never even heard of germs! Without modern science, people turned to religion and magic for answers.

Fast Fact

Dutchman Hans Lippershey designed the first telescope in 1608. That's one year after the first colonists reached Jamestown, Virginia.

Colonists used oxen, horses, and crude tools for farming.

RELIGION AND MAGIC

The colonial world was a world of mystery, superstition, and magic. Most American colonists believed that blue skies and sunshine meant that God was pleased. But when lightning struck, it was the devil's work. When crops failed, animals died, or children got sick, colonists also blamed dark forces.

superstition—a belief or idea not based on reason or knowledge

Colonists had little understanding of outer space. Many farmers believed that the moon had magical powers. They thought that a full moon pulled plants upward. This was good for beans, but bad for root vegetables such as carrots and potatoes. Farmers planted those vegetables when the moon was not full.

Strange Superstitions

There was no shortage of strange superstitions in the American colonies. Some German colonists believed that if they backed a newly purchased pig into its pen, it would stay healthy. Many Swedish colonists tried to prevent rain during harvest by saying the Lord's Prayer backward. Some colonists gave their children necklaces made of wolf fangs to help them overcome fear.

WITCHES

God and the devil were not the only supernatural forces that colonists believed in. People in Virginia, Maryland, and New England believed in witches. Witches were blamed for all kinds of misfortunes, from illnesses and deaths to property damage and even strange noises.

When something bad happened, people accused their neighbors of witchcraft. Most of the people accused were women. They were sent to prison and put on trial. Male religious leaders often served as judges.

A Report written by John Hale in 1702:

"In 1647 or 1648, a woman of Charlestown was suspected of being a witch, partly because after an argument between her and her neighbors, some mischief befell her neighbors' animals and belongings; partly because when the neighbors burned some things they thought were bewitched, the woman came to the fire and seemed concerned.

The day of her execution, I went with some neighbors who took great pains to bring her to confession and repentance. But she constantly professed herself innocent of that crime."

[Text has been changed for clarity.]

Fast Fact

The Salem witch trials were depicted in Arthur Miller's play *The Crucible*.

During the 1600s, hundreds of people were accused of witchcraft. Many were found innocent. But between 1647 and 1663, at least 10 people in New England were put to death for witchcraft.

Salem Witch Trials

The most famous witch trials occurred in Salem, Massachusetts, in 1692. A group of young girls claimed that several women had hurt them and caused them to act strangely. Over time the girls accused other people of being witches. By 1693, 19 people in the Salem area had been put to death for witchcraft. Many colonists were shocked by the trials in Salem. They began to question the belief in witches. People started to look for other causes to explain everyday problems.

Chapter 2

Looking to SCIENCE

Colonists worked together with their hands and simple tools to build ships.

Most colonists didn't realize it, but they used practical science every day. In America, the land, weather, and resources were different than in Europe. Colonists used basic **engineering** skills to build houses, roads, and ships. They also learned new ways to get salt, tan leather, and turn **iron ore** into metal.

engineering—a type of science used in construction and building

iron ore—a rough version of the metal iron

Colonists learned how to **preserve** meat with salt and smoke. American Indians taught them how to make jerky as well. Jerky is meat cut into very thin slices and dried over a slow fire. It lasts for months.

Jerky was easy to save and store for times when meat was scarce.

preserve—to protect something so that it stays in its original condition

Keeping Time

Throughout the colonial period (1607–1776) clocks were unreliable. Colonial clocks were usually about 10 minutes behind or ahead of the actual time. Clocks were powered by springs. They began slowing down unless they were rewound often. Only the very wealthy had watches. Farmers and travelers relied on the sun to provide a general idea of the time.

Though many people were superstitious in the 1600s, educated people had begun to take steps into modern science. English **philosopher** Sir Francis Bacon once declared, "knowledge is power." He encouraged people to study the world around them. Sir Isaac Newton followed that advice when he noticed an apple falling from a tree. Why did it fall? He developed the idea that **gravity** pulled things toward the center of the Earth. This kind of scientific discovery was part of a new way of thinking called the **enlightenment**.

Sir Francis Bacon was a scientist, a philosopher, and a politician.

philosopher—a person who studies truth, wisdom, knowledge, and the nature of reality

gravity—a force that pulls all things toward the center of the Earth

enlightenment—the time in the 1600s and 1700s when people turned from superstition to human reason to understand the world

Many artists have depicted Newton discovering the Law of Gravity.

In the 1600s, science was called natural philosophy.

The enlightenment eventually reached America. Some people held on to superstitious beliefs. But educated colonists turned to science. At first colonists used science to solve practical problems. They studied the soil, plants, and wildlife of America. They learned which crops grew best. They learned which reptiles were poisonous. They began to understand the climate. This study of science helped them survive.

Chapter 3

COLONIAL Medicine

Ships arriving in the colonies brought people suffering from deadly diseases.

Few serious diseases existed in America before Europeans arrived. Diseases such as smallpox, typhoid fever, and influenza came from Europe. Smallpox caused chills, fever, and terrible pus-filled blisters. It spread quickly from person to person. Typhoid fever was spread through infected food and water. Influenza, or the flu, spread through coughing, sneezing, or talking. These illnesses threatened the lives of many colonists.

Sick colonists turned to doctors. But sometimes doctors were little help. During the 1600s and early 1700s, anyone could claim to be a doctor. These people had never heard of germs or viruses. Doctors didn't bother to wash their hands before and after treating patients.

Advice on how to cure smallpox and other fevers, given to Governor Winthrop of Connecticut in 1643:

"In the month of March, fill a clay pot half full of toads. Cover it firmly, then turn it upside down and put it into a fire. Let the fire burn until it burns out. When the pot is cold, remove the toads. Pound them into a powder, and give them as medicine to the sick."

[Text has been changed for clarity.]

Fast Fact

Smallpox killed more than half of the American Indians in colonial America. Many caught the disease from European fur traders before most colonists arrived. That's why the Pilgrims found deserted villages.

Most patients were bled until they became faint or unconcious.

BAD BLOOD

Colonial doctors mistakenly believed that bad blood caused illness. To cure illnesses, doctors bled their patients. They cut into a vein and drained some of a patient's blood into a bowl. This practice often did more harm than good. If patients lost too much blood, they died.

Doctors also believed that vomiting and diarrhea carried illness out of the body. Doctors used strange ingredients to make patients vomit. People believed that the worse the medicine smelled, the more powerful it was. Some doctors added burnt leather, feathers, and a stinky plant nicknamed "devil's dung" to medicine.

Colonial doctors made their own medicines out of herbs and other common ingredients.

Doctors had strange remedies for many medical problems. Leeches were used to suck out infected blood. To cure frostbite, one doctor suggested boiling cow dung in milk and then applying it to the injury. Another doctor recommended mixing a powder of crabs' eyes with vinegar to help heal broken bones.

Fast Fact

In the South, planters' wives often provided medical care. These women had no training. They used the advice given in medical books sent from Europe.

American Indians performed dances they believed would bring healing to the body and the spirit.

NATIVE MEDICINE

Many American Indian tribes used prayer, drums, and dance to frighten away evil spirits that they believed caused illness. Native healers also used plants to treat illnesses and injuries. Many of these plants had real healing qualities.

The Eastern Woodland Indians used more than 170 different plant medicines. They ground up cherry tree bark to make cough syrup. They washed wounds with oak tree bark to prevent infections. Some of these medicines are still used today. The Delaware used dogwood to reduce fever. Sassafras or poplar bark helped heal wounds and rashes.

American Indians found healing properties in many different types of tree bark.

The sweat lodge was a common feature among most American Indain tribes.

Even though they didn't know about germs, most American Indians washed regularly. Mothers also bathed babies every day. Many tribes used hot, steamy lodges, called sweat lodges, to cure illness. People worked up a sweat singing and chanting. Then they ran outside and plunged into cold water to wash away the sweat. The cure worked for sore bones and muscles. But gathering together in sweat lodges also helped spread European diseases that killed many American Indians.

CHILDBIRTH AND CHILDREN

In both American Indian and colonial villages, there were women who served as midwives. These women helped during childbirth. Mothers gave birth at home. Female family members and neighbors often provided support. The father was not allowed to be present for a baby's birth.

The birth of a child was a cause for celebration in the colonies.

Most colonial women had five to eight children. Some women had as many as 20 and lived to an old age. However, about one in eight women died during childbirth. Many children died young as well. In some towns, three in 10 children died of fevers, smallpox, or flu. Even in the healthiest communities, one in 10 children died before age 5.

Fast Fact

There were many superstitions about childbirth. Some people believed that if a pregnant woman looked at the moon, her child would become a sleepwalker.

Hold the Soap!

Regular washing and bathing could have prevented some illnesses. But colonists thought that bathing was unhealthy. They believed that dirt provided a protective layer for their bodies. Even face-washing was unusual. Colonists believed hot water was dangerous. Cool water was only a little bit safer.

Chapter 4

SCIENCE Creeps Forward

Doctors were among the first colonists to turn to science for answers. In 1735 doctors in Boston formed a medical **society**. Doctors in New York and Charleston followed. By the mid-1700s, most colonies required doctors to have **licenses**. The first medical college was established in Philadelphia in 1765.

Colonists found many local plants could be used as medicine.

Doctors took a tip from American Indians and began studying the medicinal qualities of plants. John Bartram of Pennsylvania is considered America's first **botanist**. He traveled throughout the colonies collecting seeds and writing reports about trees, plants, and animals. He sent many seeds to scientists in London, England. As colonial explorers moved inland, they discovered even more unusual plants and animals.

society—a large group of people who have similar interests, activities, and traditions

license—a document that gives official permission to do something

botanist—a scientist who studies plants

STUDYING SCIENCE

By the mid-1700s, educated Americans recognized that science could provide useful answers to everyday problems. Botany was one of the first sciences to capture people's interest. Soon people also began studying animals and rocks and minerals.

In 1743 Benjamin Franklin organized the American Philosophical Society. Doctors, lawyers, ministers, and businessmen joined the society to discuss important scientific ideas. George Washington, John Adams, Thomas Jefferson, and Alexander Hamilton were members of this group.

Many of America's founding fathers were part of the American Philosophical Society.

In 1768 Adam Kuhn taught the first college course in botany at the College of Philadelphia. Other colleges such as Harvard, William and Mary, Yale, and Princeton also added science courses. Astronomy, the study of stars and planets, became especially popular. Newly formed libraries increased scientific learning. Slowly, but surely, American science was moving forward.

BEN FRANKLIN, COLONIAL SCIENTIST

Franklin was the most famous scientist in the colonies. He was also a respected politician and inventor. In 1747 he began studying lightning. Franklin began a series of famous experiments using a key attached to a kite. His experiments led to greater understanding of electricity. Armed with information about how lightning works, Franklin invented the lightning rod. It helps prevent house fires. The lightning rod carries lightning away from a house and into the ground.

Fast Fact

Benjamin Franklin was quoted as saying, "If you would not be forgotten, as soon as you are dead and rotten, either write things worth reading, or do things worth the writing."

Franklin had many other scientific interests. He studied magnets, ship design, and the connection between sweating and body temperature. Franklin invented bifocals. These eyeglasses allow people to see near and far objects clearly. He also invented the Franklin stove, which heated a home better than a fireplace.

BECOMING A SCIENTIFIC NATION

America's many self-taught scientists began to record their ideas and experiment with new inventions. Franklin encouraged this attitude toward science. So did Thomas Jefferson. Jefferson believed that human progress and happiness depended on science and invention. He read about plants, weather, astronomy, geology, and other sciences. He conducted scientific experiments and worked on inventions throughout his life.

Transit of Venus

In the 1760s, scientists around the world began preparing for a transit of Venus. A transit of Venus occurs when the planet Venus, viewed from Earth, crosses the sun. Two transits occur eight years apart, and then not again for 100 years. A transit occurred in 1761 and 1769. American scientist David Rittenhouse built a special clock and telescope which he used to study the 1769 transit. He carefully recorded his observations. Rittenhouse's notes earned him worldwide respect.

The *American Turtle* failed in its attempt to bomb the British ship H.M.S. *Eagle*.

An increase in scientific study wasn't the only change happening in colonial America. In 1776 the colonies declared their independence from Great Britain. That same year David Bushnell built a submarine named *American Turtle*. It was the first submarine to ever attack an enemy target. Other inventions followed. So did expanded study in many areas of science. Americans had turned away from superstition and toward reason and knowledge. Science was leading them into a bright new future.

GLOSSARY

botanist (BAH-tuh-nist)—a scientist who studies plants

engineering (en-juh-NEER-ing)—a type of science used in construction and building

enlightenment (en-LITE-uhn-muhnt)—the time during the 1600s and 1700s when people turned from superstition to human reason to understand the world

gravity (GRAV-uh-tee)—a force that pulls objects together; gravity pulls objects down toward the center of Earth and the moon

iron ore (EYE-urn OR)—a rough version of the metal iron

license (LYE-suhnss)—a document that gives official permission to do something

philosopher (fuh-LOSS-uh-fur)—a person who studies truth, wisdom, knowledge, and the nature of reality

preserve (pri-ZURV)—to protect something so that it stays in its original state

society (suh-SYE-uh-tee)—a large group of people who have similar interests, activities, and traditions

superstition (soo-pur-STI-shuhn)—a belief or idea not based on reason or knowledge

READ MORE

Fishkin, Rebecca Love. *English Colonies in America.* We The People. Minneapolis: Compass Point Books, 2009.

Kalman, Bobbie. *A Visual Dictionary of a Colonial Community.* Crabtree Visual Dictionaries. New York: Crabtree Pub. Co., 2008.

Raum, Elizabeth. *The Dreadful, Smelly Colonies: The Disgusting Details about Life During Colonial America.* Disgusting History. Mankato, Minn.: Capstone Press, 2010.

INTERNET SITES

FactHound offers a safe, fun way to find Internet sites related to this book. All of the sites on FactHound have been researched by our staff.

Here's all you do:

Visit *www.facthound.com*

Type in this code: 9781429661409

 Check out projects, games and lots more at
www.capstonekids.com

INDEX

PRIMARY SOURCE BIBLIOGRAPHY

Page 8—as published in *Narratives of the New England Witchcraft Cases, 1648–1706*, edited by George Lincoln Burr (New York: Scribner, 1914.)

Page 15—as published in *A History of American Life*, edited by Arthur M. Schlesinger and Dixon Ryan Fox (New York: Macmillan, 1927.)

Page 23—as published in *Science and Its Times, Vol. 4: 1700–1799*, (Farmington Hills, Michigan: Gale Group, 2001.)

Page 27—as written in a letter to Dr John Mitchel F.R.S. dated April 29, 1749.